Everyone A Bell

Everyone A Bell

Poems by

S. B. Merrow

Cover art by Ana Kolega

Cover design by Shay Culligan

ISBN: 978-1-950462-71-1

Kelsay Books Inc.

kelsaybooks.com

502 S 1040 E, A119
American Fork, Utah 84003

for my loves,

Robert, Jessie, Duncan, and Alma

Acknowledgments

With deep gratitude to the editors of the following journals and presses who first published these poems, sometimes as earlier versions, or with different titles.

Bay to Ocean, The Year's Best Writing from the Eastern Shore: "Returning"

Broad River Review: "Bricolage," "Autumn Rot"

The Courtship of Winds: "The Narrow Land," "3. Totality"

Free State Review: "A Puddle of Glitter on the Top of My House," "The 100th Birthday Party"

Gyroscope Review: "The Seed Vault," "After A Spat," "Sherwood Gardens"

Naugatuck River Review: "Bicycling Sharpsburg"

Nimrod International Journal: "Craving"

Panoply: "Offshore"

Passager: "Natural Order," "Time Travel"

Plainsongs Magazine: "Ellipses"

Quill's Edge Press chapbook *Unpacking the China:* "Unpacking the China," "Mother," "Gladiator," "Pan's Questions," "Ghosts," "The Carp Lie Still," "Building A House Beside Three Trees," "When You're 64," "A Becoming Place"

Reflections, 100 Years of Friendship and Hiking at AMC Cold River Camp: "Mabel's Dam"

The River: "Camp Skit in Five Parts"

Salamander Magazine: "Big Old"

Tishman Review: "For Husbands," "Growing Things"

WORDPEACE: "Reading *Half-Earth,* "Blossom"

The author wishes to thank Barrett Warner, who helped prepare this collection, Kendra Kopelke for her editorial suggestions, *Vox Populi* and Michael Simms for showcasing some of these poems, poets Kathy Mangan, Kathleen Shemer, Katy Burke Stanton, Lalita Norontha, Shirley Brewer, David Bergman, and Mary Ann McFadden for their advice and encouragement, and Karen Kelsay for saying yes, and publishing this book.

Contents

I

The 100th Birthday Party

Those who could make the party
on Route One arrived exhausted—
uncles, brothers, friends, some of them

already deceased. Admit it,
everyone has a difficult journey.
Former in-laws were there,

and a few lovers of ex-lovers
—my photographer and his—someone
to chronicle the humor and heartbreak.

I decorated with twisted ribbons
and hoped for a celebration of long life,
the many paths—religious or not—

toward something we call peace.
I'm not naive, but I thought maybe
the haters had all died off.

I'm afraid it ended in a brawl
when folks decided to say out loud
everything they long had felt.

It wasn't that bad. I watched the replay,
huddled with your camera
as people started to leave, guided

by the children who cried
like chicks: *pio, pio, pio,*
cuando tienen hambre, cuando tienen frio.

The old man remained at the party,
settled in his barbed spine,
time's noisy labyrinth,

until finally, we had a space to talk,
hearts open to the sky. Would
our last words have been kinder

if we'd stayed on that mountain
where every living thing does
only what it must to survive?

.

Bricolage

Long ago, you adopted a raptor—
with a tinker's charm, you
summoned its generous wings.
For years you rolled down
bumpy streets, gathering

ornaments, nonsense, heartbeats
of rain in the bed of your truck,
the laughter of horses.
You were ravenous for clarity
and longing to soar.

You wore a coat of crazy
colors, a black bib below
your rusty beard. 'Nothing to fear,'
you said, polishing the pots,
steady as a clock. Then, we

found the feathers in your pocket,
banded, spotted, yellow and black
—meaning something to you—
a mutilated flicker in the last
town you rambled through.

Ellipses

When no means *no*
until it means *yes,*
words are sacrifice,
tongues for the starving,
bright sour things
to suck in gratitude,
offered in minor keys
that mock the moment.

Nothing is clear
except its opposite—
voices of *miel* sticky as facts
and true so rarely you ask
why now and in what language?

But there they lie
like light on the sheet,
airy and entering
lands you've never seen,
and before you can cry
no! not this . . .
they sing you back
with animal songs,
your first memories
of the naked choir.

Grammie's Beasts

Grandma Higgins came to the house
after mass on Christmas Day holding
a tin of perfect cashews and our tickets
to see the famous Lippizans
performing in a bowl of sawdust
lifting high their red-clad riders
on stiffly dancing legs

Grammie kept her mane in place
with hairpins made of dead tortoises
I longed to touch but never did
the piled swirls of gray-gold taffy
and something darker (like mine now)
if it fell free I never saw
even that morning arriving early

for a drive to Rockport's shops
to feast on clams at Oleana's—
her pearls lay coiled like sleeping snakes
silk stockings on the shower rod
I stood between the brocade chair
—a wingéd giant with lion claws—
and the ivory bank of her piano

I was a cheeky, naughty seventeen
when I glanced up and caught her eye
in the dresser mirror—we were two predators
intimate with sin—
she plucked a stray hair from her chin
then arranged her combs again
in their handsome nest

Mabel's Dam

for the Moffettes

Cold River tumbles
     the striated quartz granite
          below Mabel's dam,

white over white, a saga
     of stream and local folk,
          of rages gathered and

coiled against confining banks
     where force found its pattern,
          carving anger into bowls

in the bedrock. In 1923,
     Mabel's father built a dam
          in her memory. Women

with buckets and brooms
     swept the newly bared
          depressions, filled them

again from the flow—their babies
     played and bathed
          here where we sit

below the dam, rapids shooting
     the chutes, shaping channels
          for our thoughts, waves

that crest in mid-river, glint like ice
     then slide back,
          remaining in place.

Mother

Mother had slender hands
but something about her eyes
held me off, some old outrage
cleaving face from heart
—it sounds painful I know—
a double wound, if you count mine.

More queen than mother hen,
she knew choice might lead to wonder
or worse, to wonder why.
I rested my head below her collar,
the ramparts of her jaw
above, high enough to deflect
anyone firing upon the throne.

There were thrills, though,
swimming in high ponds
with leaf litter and waterbugs,
undressing on an evergreen bank
like Daphnis and Penelope,
a silent duet so white I thought
we would draw fire were there snipers around
—was that who we feared?

Gladiator

They wear hairpins
dipped in my blood

and flowers of spring
to soothe the wounds

where memory lives,
a visible soul

that crawls out face-first
to behold itself.

Who is in charge here?
Behind her chariot

the sea of arena-bound
run hip to hip,

breasts exposed,
spears in hand,

the expert and the untried
—oh, the color!—

And beasts still spin
beyond the door,

hungry wild.

Janie and I

lobbed balsam-stuffed
          pillows over the hard-
     wood sea splitting

our bedspreaded nations, the islands of
          our sisterhood,
     paisley cats

begging to be hurled.
          We played until monsters
     rose on the wall,

my sister fearless
          with Downs' syndrome chucking
     her pungent missile

at shadows. I ducked and
          grabbed the scented air.
     Throwing

with abandon and a guffaw
          I envied,   Jane
     seemed both

older and younger,
     a fragile leader.   Feathery
          hair, delicate fingers floated

untroubled when she ran
          and I flung with care, with
     a child's ken of weakness.

I last heard her laugh when
          she was fifty-five. She was
     in bed again.

We had walked too far in
          the fragrant fields,   me
     hunting for herbs

feverfew boneset something
          for the heart.   She was
     touching her chest

in surprise, knew
          I'd landed   a good one
     right there.

The Seed Vault

In my dream, baby goats
are hopping all over time. Hey, kids!
I shout, ecstatic with the promise
of new beginnings

hopping all over time. Hey, kids!
In white silence we bounce around
the hillside, jostling between
thought and sleep in our taut glee.

In white silence we bounce around
dreaming, and I wonder what
the trees would say, black branches
tossing in the night. No longer

dreaming, I wonder what other
joy could be this quiet, maybe
seeds on ice in an arctic vault,
waiting out the rain.

Navigation

After years floating and mute,
I again found the star
poised in the north.

I had been backstroking at dusk,
aiming straight for the island,
a swimmer without a marker
but for the party-sounds there,
bright over water.

Arriving after dark, cold
and aching for the light on their faces,
I paused before scaling the rocks,
at rest in my body the boat
for this crazy journey
of naked churning,

and met the *dueño* of the shore,
cool skinned dauphin, his whispers
like waves, mushroom-wise
—before I turned around, sinking
back, ears in the lake.

And there was Polaris,
sun of someone's days but
better at night, and constant.

Time Travel

I imagined you, willowy boy,
back on the summer island
—*so crunchy,* you sneered,
all wispy blond beard & swagger,
your slang a signal those last days
you'd moved on for the year,
fixed on another girl's anklet.

Then I saw you down by the water,
though you live in another state
and forty years are spent—
long-necked and free, sandy haired,
unhurrying towards the boats.

Who *is* he, the youth I passed,
so certain of you, your
gesture and scent? So now
we are three, sparking
the hay-wired terrain of first love.

Would you be roused, too,
or is he my synaptic stray?
Not an emotion out of place
that isn't out of time.

For Husbands

Remember how we left on Day One
after the wedding, filled the hatchback
with everything we owned, and headed
for California? The top layer of our cake
remained in my parents' freezer. Before
all the penny stresses and business blahs
we were kids—we drove across Texas,
tried their steaks and King Crab, blew a tire
outside Gallup, New Mexico. Semis roared
past our car unpacked all over the desert,
the temperature a hundred and ten—
The one bedroom in the six-unit
a long block from the pier in Long Beach,
half the place usurped by the former tenant's
waterbed wherein we couldn't sleep or do
anything but bounce around together. On hot
nights I tiptoed along its frame to show off
my balance, and my tan. You ate the first
meal I learned to cook, chicken a l'orange,
and proving even kinder, you brought
meatball subs downtown when I worked
in property management at that weird place
near the *Queen Mary's* berth where, I guess
you never knew, I spotted my doppelgänger
one day. After that, I didn't manage much,
much less the small talk in that office. Once,
you got a speeding ticket from a tough city
cop spangled in navy and gold, for bicycling
faster than thirty with a Latin name.
The indignity stung, and later your brother-
in-law loaned us the new Pontiac to enjoy a sunset

from the high road above the sea—on the shoulder
you hit a broken signpost, the Firebird got mangled,
—and remember how you were forgiven?
Your sister's spaniel ate the Peruvian *huaca*
you brought back from a dig near Lima, and she
was forgiven, too. You named our terrier pup
Mr. MacIntyre after the gun-stock craftsman
out there, your friend who carved hard-wood
beauties for collectors who could pay. I don't
remember a thing about the three thousand
mile drive back to Boston, but maybe you do.
I remember the Pacific's pull on you, surfer boy
who loved that ocean and its tides, its waves
and mists a different blue, luminous, the foothills
a softer brown than anything I'd known. Surely,
breathing the air of your childhood,
we were both happy.

Pan's Questions

Not birds,
to what do we return in spring?
Why is the flute's sweetness
an echo like mist in these chambers
we choose as frost descends
and the light departs?

I recall hunting horns in winter,
waiting out storms for a flute, just one,
to balance their dove-sad cries
with a touch of pliant green—

and worship the impulse to ask, why
(as communities of viols and oboes
obsessed with their moment declaim)
does the flute question, but never
answer the dark?

Offshore

Piloting among islands, miles
of silence and fog over the grasping,
slow caress of eel grass,

I picture bulbous roots

under the ancient water, water folded
now into clouds that, crossing the fickle face of god,
pass through each other, leaking, wet.

So often out here, men end up dead,

unlucky fish in an understocked ocean.
B.B. sings their lonely blues—
sometimes I wonder, would a matchbox hold my clothes.

Who launched this flimsy boat
into the tidal struggle? We could be in Paris,
eating oysters at Gertrude's, dancing
to the crackle of fireplace music,
the descrescendo of a vibrating day.

But out here among the sailors, displaced
from landscape, our lives enlarged
by tellings

retold on mingled rivers,

we leave all reckoning
to the fog, its fluid arms
the nursemaids of form,

paddling forever, it seems,

between these shanties on the bar
and your sea-gray eyes,
my heart a salty hinge that opens.

II

Everyone A Bell

In the movie of childhood despair sounds like hope,
a cowbell maybe, that clangs every day at five.
It wasn't mentioned at supper, the clubhouse
under the porch. She was young, still
fumbling her knife—and in the end
was excused from her plate of chewed meat,
the hours she spent avoiding his eyes.

Now imagine that bell once hung from the neck
of a captive cow, how its noise assaulted
her wiry ears, her spirit unable to shrug off
the clamor and choke and fact of that weight.

Rainy days, they got out of mom's way
building forts of brown boxes. He closed
the lid and sat full down. She panicked bad
—*but it's just a game,* he calmly said
and let her out, cowboy-hatted,
for torture by tickle, Indian rope burns,
dumb beast tied to a cellar pole.

If this is a movie, it will need music
to be fit for release. I hear jazz, a quintet,
the drummer a master who tells the story
with flailing wrists—who in the mayhem
gives everyone a bell, and their moment to wail.

Reading *Half-Earth*

E.O. Wilson says that when the elephants
    die, so will we, who have sought,

seen and named 12,000 kinds of ants,
    leaf-cutters, armies, iridescent and fiery.

"The Mind of the Biosphere," we are busy
    with our big-game hunt for happiness,
        rounds of beer-pong that require focus,
sidewalks, half the earth. Humans
    shuffle to extinction, cups in hand,
        cloaked in microbes,
in sunny fealty to fickle gods,

while earthworm nations and unknown species
    settle the moist jungle, nomads in the dark.

I recycle, shut off lights and shiver.
    The future has always been uncertain, this

not-knowing as familiar as love—as *luck* —
    (to share our genes with thriving rats.)

One day, when costly measures
    yield slight progress, we will cite

the sad numbers, mention
    those poachers on the savanna.

E.O. Wilson says we already know
    what happens to elephants—to us—

when families are broken,
    matriarchs and memories gone.

Bicycling Sharpsburg

Sunken Road dapples with tree shadow, the hills a sweet
strain on morning muscles—over there, Antietam Creek,

a copper-red flow in memory of brothers who fought
for their bank at the splintered boundary of America.

We venture off the pebbled path to sit among the weeds
with southern spiders and northern ticks. Bones below

whisper the cost of one day 150 years ago with
23,000 human deaths. Cycle on, the summer sings—

it blossoms and fades without call or horn. I find water
at a barn painted with Confederate flags, feel the silent

spilling rage we can't quite hear within our frame—the real
toll of everyday murder—for selling CD's, for having

a broken taillight, for being alive and black just last week.
Cycle on the twisting road where mustards and milkweed,

choice food for monarchs, edge the field where fathers fell.
Back-lit in the slanting light, tonight's corn feeds on living soil

as children romp on monuments to waste, shoot finger pistols
into a bruise-blue distance, South Mountain echoing their cries.

Ghosts

A bell chimes and when

I open the screen, no one—
no note, no package,
an azalea jamming
the retina with pink chaos.
Pigeon-folk worry themselves silly
on the travertine steeple

yet don't think to leave.
There are globes of rain on the waxy sedum,
uneven sidewalks
already dry to the tree wells,
women on the porch where you used to live,
the usual crawl of cars.

A distant siren drags
the fallen bloodied to mind,
first clarion since the bell woke me
from my night's dim work
demanding a password
on the morning's threshold.

Graffiti Free

We go up in a hot air balloon through
a murder of crows, free in the wide gray sky
to be one spot among many escaping
together, free to caw and circle above
the auburn branches losing their trust
and free themselves to be naked, waving
last burned flags and soon to scrape out
a winter tune like a trumped-up man

on the edge of Edge City—free as a woman
to walk around in Freedom Park, to read
at Freedom School, to earn money
and keep it, free to stay, to choose desire,
or to sleep on the street living faux free
and thirsty for the real Freedom Cocktail—
our need to drink and be merry, as free
as any victim of gravity to drop to the floor

like a silver pin in a silent theater,
or to flail at our dropping, just blokes
after a brawl waiting for oblivion,
falling free and scattering like mail
through the slot in a carved wood door
you are free to unhinge.

The tracks run both ways
as we leave and see fields of wheat glinting
like scabbards, sheaths of grain swords for the free
imagination—until the last stop, end of the ride,
where the platform's filthy freedom banners
run ads and more ads on the fat man's back
just above the crack where his shirt says
"The Future is Now."

What does freedom want? To paint the walls
blood and all souls blue, plant vines of kudzu
over the land—so pretty and quick—
my conscience, free in the social noise,
answers only to strangers in this superb
moment, as freedom naps through the day
like a graffiti artist. I gather a handful

of the fallen free to hold and regard.
But among the burrs and weeds of gravity,
I cannot weigh the petals of this wild
flower or take its hairy measure, to ask
why it should belong to me—
and what does it cost?

After the Inauguration No One Attended

1. *It Wasn't a Dream*

The tide is low in Baltimore. I try to avoid
pools of too muchness, anything too
lonely—the brickwork of alcoves, slower wheels
sucking along the flats, frowns under scarves.

I fall asleep on an ambulance line, dream
the white whinnies of Pegasus en route, in flight
through a godless night, then wake to the cat's
hopeful chortles (like squeaky casters on a rug,
they alter the shape of a room in morning.)

For a minute we walk the narrow sill
together, just pussies clawing at the glass,
do as we please, until the sadness startles and,
human again, I head out to hail a cab, kindle
a chat, lob a package, maybe, onto the neighbor's
porch, or cue a mute rake over the season's leavings

to lose myself in the front garden, aware
only of shadows of seagulls that sail
from roof to gutter over the Calvert Street
canyons, out of place, almost lost.

2. *August*

We've burned the fields, bramble and toad.
Most of the birds are gone. Poetry, singed by fire,
charges even the stones with speech. Released

by the blaze, charred seeds centuries old
promise to deliver what pirates command—
unruly growth, cruel death, glorious mayhem.

Ephemeral flowers will sprout,
strangers without context, riddles
in themselves. I step into a Halal store,

drawn by the toasting snacks.
The owner brightens
when he sees my ring, a square

of lapis lazuli set in gold, a rib
of earth blue in the night—"that stone
is from my country!" he cries—I will

soon flee the mouth of the darkening cave
like a dove aching sound in flight, mourning
the scorched trees, no roost to preen or sing.

3. *Totality*

We yearn for the eclipse,
something new—a corona,
flares to rekindle hope, banana-
shaped visions, another decade.

Truckers pull off the highway
to watch the haunting shadows.
Beyond the shoulder, golfers
stop playing their game.

A woman from California
gives us special glasses and
talks about her dying father,
how moving home would mean

divorce. She declares the event
over before it is. We walk
a woodsy path sprinkled with
sun-sickles, the grating cicadas

mute. Farther south, it turns
dark—whippoorwhills wake
and sing as if morning will
never come. Then, across the country,

the brief night of totality passes.
Back in our parallel lanes,
we marvel at the speed
of disappearing dreams.

The Carp Lie Still

The carp lie still in the pond,
and cattle descend the meadow.
Crickets hum of darkness and it's time to pray
in the Church of the Second Amendment.
BAM! BAM! Muskrat, oak, fern and snake—
recoil in a unison of fear.

He wants what is unseen, a wary
solidity touched by grace
—or a deer in the thickets.
BAM! bawls his fathomless need,
twisted din in the pelvis.

A joke to think he might
step out of the laurel with his talking stick
and a prayer of thanks, maybe for life,
but at least for death—rather,
there's a thorny scramble up the power line
to hurl another handful of ammo at the woods
and be left more alone than a god
whose pockets are empty of thunderbolts.

BAM YOU! Crazed altar boys
end the birdsong vespers, pounding the hills
with gunfire from sea to shining sea.

What's natural about this, I ask Hera's daughters,
girls in the cafe standing ready to serve
with a shrug and a sigh, and a want
of freedom in the hollow of their bodies,
their own anger keeping the supper warm.

Camp Skit in Five Parts

Wherein
A White Woman   Plays Dead   To See Where It Gets Her

(Breathe)

Part I. Wherein The Lion Lays Down with the Lamb

We Have a Late Breakfast of Potatoes
With Some Kind of Fowl Wrapped in Pale Cabbage
Funny That Today The Food is So White!
Two Campers Argue About Politics,
Resolve Their Differences By Playing Guitar
One of Them is a Big Deal in Russia They Say
But It's Summer and We're Here To Disengage

(Breathe)

Part II. Wherein I Go for a Dip in the Lake

10 AM Gray Sky Wild Whitecaps
A Floating Brown Basket Shaped Like a Ship
Sinks Within a Stone's Throw of the Shore
I Watch it Go Down
Jump In to Rescue   Swim Towards the Bottom
The Ship's Dark Shadow—and Bones are Scattered
Across the Lake Floor   Broken Legs   and Jaws
Horse Heads   and   Various Skulls
All of Them White

(Surfacing, Breathe)

Part III. Wherein Our Rickety Docks Have All Been Rebuilt

Impervious Lumber on the Roughest of Footings
Strange Men Talking Guard the Piers and
Block my Emergence from the Water
Keeping Head Down Thighs Tight
I Lift and Move Their Arms Aside
Squeeze Past Dripping Wet
My Skin Prickly White

(Breathe)

Part IV. On the Main Path

The New Crowd Threatens Us with AR-15s
A Friend With a Stare Warns Me to Stand Still
Resisting I Run and Am Stopped By Someone
Who Shoots Through a Pillow and Misses Me
Just Play Dead and See How It Goes
I Crawl to the Edge of a Staircase
And Down
Where A Woman With Rifle Notices
The "Innocent" Play Dead Again
She Lays Her Hand on My Back Until

(Breathe)

Part V. My Face White with Fear I Have to Breathe

Go Ahead Play Dead—and See Where It Gets You

End

Building A House Beside Three Trees

bucket and scoop
the question of where
to drop displace discard
old earth never exposed to sun
racing rain to finish neat
nail guns flail before wind
jump ladder thread beam
hang tarp shovel to the end
then push prevails
and shout bang team wins
in seven days eight men
raise three stories footing to gable
windows plumbing locks
wired for man

while fingers of maple in flower

caress new roofs
adapt without sound
(thousands of hushed
buds defer complaint)
roots severed trunks
tense they bank patience
on slow future
of leaf-litter sun showers
humans free of malice
and the drama passes
like raising a flag
a morning ceremony
built on emptiness where space
seemed to rule though
their majesty asks us now
to love more the silence

III

A Puddle of Glitter on the Roof of My House

I spotted a comet among the clouds
behind the gargoyles of St. John's, and waited
for the sky to open, to record the visitation.

Here was a new vein of quicksilver, beyond
the reach of your fancy phone, like transcribing
a solo of Oscar Peterson with the ear of an ant.

I breathed a few bars into my bag and,
for good measure, stitched a velvet star
onto the back flap of *Loving Frank* on
the morning train, not able to abandon
Mamah in her strife and worldly pain.

Once home, after the chopping and roasting
of dinner, I unpacked my purse and found
a trajectory of notation on the lining. That
night, I installed apparati on the roof. This

was not easy, you understand. Help me
to capture the Comet of St. John's, I prayed
to the lonely gods, who watched hopefully.

If I wrestle (to my death) its powerful tail, at least
I'll have known the dragon star's icy tongue
and scales of dust, seasonal muse.

Frances of Dun Chaoin

A gale blew up from nowhere, strafing
the treeless asphalt. At the intersection, I thought
I glimpsed the heavy loop of her gray braid,
her inner gaze on the sea-side flora
of another plain. She walked the bohareen
alone, tiny forests at her feet, alert for toothed
or lanced or penny shapes—for pinwheels,
cats' ear, ling—heeding the sticky, hairy stalks,
the woody, ropy, glabrous growth,
each minute newly moist under a sky
in passage through the four seasons.
Had we been closer and the wind more generous
with its secret, I'd have seen reflected in her eyes
a fan of sea-spray above the Kerry cliff.

Desire

is spacious at sixty,
a brook swollen with rain
like piano arpeggios,

an evening with Oban
on a freshly swept porch,
sparrow chirp, cat quiver,

a walk at night in cool grass,
the roots below the clasping stalks
dew-soaked and lacy,

the way we jest as you brush
the mud from shoes with
your impatient hands.

When You're 64

Mornings in bed talk is an ocean,
its swells and troughs the waters of life
where we are held and rocked,
the other, the only here.

Were there a perfect sound
would it pulse like passing trains
or wingbeats, and weep with the man
by the brook, by the trout lilies?

Would we find a perfect shape
with eyes or hands, and know it
surely as in a dream, as a still life,
or as a schooner made of clay?

Were love perfect, would it be fixed
in marble or in ice? Would it swim
and float among all other strengths
at the same time we work at

only listening? Here in the room
where inside meets outside
and morning walks the roofline,
I am the ark and the dove on your arm,

and will still need you, still feed you.

Unpacking the China

One piece survived the Civil War, and obviously,
so did its women. I hold on to dishes—
among us survivors, I alone like them.
They're pretentious I'm told, and odd.
Harbored high on the back shelf,
a few sidle to the front—the plate of gilded lattice,
a Moorish tile Grammie carried home in her case.
My favorite is the most useless,
not the painted teapot that holds twelve ounces,
though it's pointless enough
for these magnum days of our undoing.
The fifty-seven kitchen cupboards have unmoored me
thanks to Costco, or whoever out there calculates
the size of my grip or my stomach, my family,
the shape of my life basically,
something they have no business thinking about.
No, I love the crystal bowl with its notched rim,
half-inch walls carved with foliage
and peonies, forever in bloom.
Tap it anywhere with anything
to sound one resonant note.
We buy Tibetan Singing Bowls,
aural immortality for twenty-five dollars at the fair
—but the one note, cool as the moon,
recalls every phase, remembers
much more than you or I.

Autumn Rot

Here's rooting for decay in
the siren-flamed sunshine
where pavement cracks grow
weeds, rats caper at fences,
and a bony stray naps on the porch
we decided not to paint this year,
something about decrepitude
and alley aesthetics....

We're all a little desiccated
after the season's earthquake,
downpours, wind and heat,
but now it's the sprout, the leap,
the sleeping in the sun that's key,
eyelids low, breathing the rank
and rubbery twitch of leaf-death.

The same bright river that spills
from distant peaks and smooths
the jagged erratics of an ice age
we've all heard about

makes its way to the falls
via this lane named Lovegrove,
a back street storm drain,

reshaping permanence—
and puny words our tools,
unlike the rats' and the weeds'—
as rock becomes river
that carves the canyon.
En route, it sunders us, too.

After A Spat

Never too drunk to knit a sock,
               cinch yarn around needle and *tug*
        on the double-wrapped stitches,

those holes at the ankle that
               keep coming around,
        row after row, intractable. They *will*

be tacked shut. Place glass,
               good and empty, on floor
        to catch the ivy's persistent drips—

click-clacks singing "hydrated, hy-dray-ted,"
               while a farmer's wife
        hacks blindly at mice.

Cast yarn at the next pointed stick
               (fiercely as possible
        at two a.m.,) then the next, for

there's always a point. Just knit
               and repeat the pattern,
        oh man, the mad pattern.

Blossom

It's cicada-time
     and treetops are buzzing.
I take a walk on a narrow road,
busier avenues roaring
with commuters, honking trucks,
my padded footsteps the one
soft sound—this blue-speared
chicory was not here yesterday,
I think, recalling the ways
and everything that we forget—

the million gems
     beneath our street,
          green serpentine, amethyst—
the way a low sun scrapes
across damp grasslands, the tallest clumps
        shining like beacons—
the fact that our lives are seasonal brooks,
     shallow and flowing, for now—

when a skinny man
approaches with a limp and a cane,
then turns around to walk the other way,
looks over his shoulder and calls to me
"you ever get turned around ass-backwards,
forget which alley you're on?"
Hibiscus flower on a slender stalk,
his smile blossoms pink and wide.

The Water We Breathe

*—on the opening at the Baltimore Museum of Art, featuring works
of Tomás Saraceno and Annet Couwenberg*

Everyone wears black. Someone
          is talking about the long-lived earth
    and we pretend to comprehend.

The artist fingers her creation—
          a river of damask on the wall, bony
    sturgeons in a blue underworld. Across

the gallery, we enter the spider's web, spotlight
          on our boundaries. Servers passing
    gulps of wine empty their silver trays.

The women display, men navigate the
          confident air. They all
    bypass the musicians, stationed by dessert.

Even so, the flutist grows taller
          with each breath. The music rises, too,
    up the blushing columns, a kaleidoscope

of leaping fishes on the rippled ceiling.

Big Old

Heron fishes midstream,
    wading as through
        a time slower than
           the Susquehanna's
        hours upon years
    upon stone,   so when
he flies I almost panic
    after all this time
        in the shallows,

           colors floating by,
        Canada geese paddling
    upended and submerged,
cormorants diving for long seconds
    and we're alone
        where shad and darters
           once thrived, a place
             of mills and sloops,
        that is, before
    the railroad and dam and
river-bottom black sludge.

        Glad he was here
      on his dripping stilts,
    until reasons to leave
rippled past.

A Becoming Place

A pop-up wilderness west of the Piedmont,
folded land of sudden impediments
scored by creeks and runs,
and linked by bird and folk
to well-spaced cousins
in the north, where brooks
gather sunlight from the peaks.

I saw them first from 10,000 feet up—
feral cats asleep on a furry map,
their muscles glinting in the sloping sun,
snow on pale underbellies
offered briefly to fingers,
rough coats dark and uncombed
in colonies of recumbent order
soft in the winter light.

But these silted hollows—
cloaked in poplar and paw paw
between the restless ridges
consigned to faux youth
in their half-height—
tease and pluck at my dislocation.

I puzzle this stronghold
of the Green Man, ancient fool
untamed by culture, until a switchback
deposits me on the Potomac plain
like a raft of last year's leaves.

Glimpsed through trunks,
the silver river drags its world

as a coal train on the far bank
creeps upstream. Velocities match,
vectors cancel. Road, river, and mountain
pause beside a house
where somebody felt what I feel
and said, *I could settle here.*

IV

Craving

What I want is just one chance to be inside your life.
Not to share the same supper, to learn the good news before

your favorite sister, and I don't mean the kind of understanding
that comes after lovers decide to scuttle their fear, lie together

and find in time the meaning of art, or children, though that
will be good enough, working it all out in the morning

over two bowls of cereal dotted with blueberries, fine dark stars
in a milky cosmos, one for almost every dip of the spoon.

I'm talking about a night we spend in the same body on the
same smooth stones on the bottom of the dry river
                    when a storm comes.

Our two ears wake to the sound of rushing water, hearing
as in a duet the same whoosh before we are seized
                    by the waist and

for the first time my skin is your skin, submerged and invisible,
as we are dragged by the legs, scraping our back, our mouth
                    full of sand,

my mind yours in its urge to swim. It happens fast, like magic,
though I'm not sure I grasp, even then, what it is to be you.

The Narrow Land

Magic is an unmarked place,
              guarded by children
                      racing roller-skates over cracked sidewalks
      pursued by chocolate wolves
                      with cherry maws, uniformed cops
                      —or heedless adults
                              already up to their hips
                                  in joy.
These are dangerous waters
                  you're doomed to dream
              because you are human and too timid to stare
                      long at the bum selling you
                              the depth of his gaze.

            But enter and sight sharpens,
        chatter runs fast backwards. You see
    a narrow land
        alive with wavy water games,
              dotted with emerald and gold
                      cottages without attics.

            At the end of the beach,
    bracketed by cliffs
                  cut with ancient stairs
                      cobbled without mortar,
                  vines of red bougainvillea
                          rise in the heat and sparkle.
                          Come winter,
                      the chasm will drip with
                  prisms, a painting in azure and ice,
              the firs up top
        stunted with longing.

Cabin on the Town Line

People picnic by the river after days
      of heavy rain. One outgoing
            woman, winking, married,

tells me she's bisexual, that my smell
      is sweetfern. Are the boundaries
            one person feels and another sees

anything like this
      New England town's three-hundred-year-
            old stone walls—their fluid

sense of time, chipmunk-fast play-
      spaces lichen-slow to change?
            These folks knew

how to build, and when to stop—
      the outhouse placed as far from the kitchen
            as possible & still inside the line,

is up against the mossy boulders. Walking
      the path on moon-filled nights, I can
            make out just how far

the bearberry has wandered this year. And
      how about that pyramid of quartz
            thirty feet over into Halifax

standing up to the prideful air, the forest,
      the interrupted ferns—pristinely white
            and at a height you can't miss

when upstairs and upright
        at the window, making love—
                not a mortal in sight.

A hurricane detoured Silver Brook
        a few years back. Anything
                but silver after all this rain—

the chocolatey stream of silt and soil,
        the edge of its world a blur, moves
                the hillside tree by stone, tumbles

any rock begging a rest. But of course
        it will subside. Dragonflies light
                to dry their wings, sedges

send roots to a new shore—we tell stories
        and pass the salads
                as clouds disperse.

The Carpenter

The edge of his desk is sharp on my wrist,
    —from here, we can't see
        whatever it is that holds us up.

The carpenter left his bevel
    unsoftened. I picture in mind
        his hands on the wood—

it happens sometimes when the wind
    blows wild, the scent of sawdust
        gone. A voice recorder

lies on the table. My father held it
    and managed the buttons
        at ninety-three

to speak of how, when he was a boy,
    he and a friend built a Snipe
        and sailed the boat

around and around the Mystic Lakes.
    There were only a few leaks,
        he said.

Returning

Working the breeze, the patterns
it makes high on a shapely canvas
where small flutters tell

of perfect tension, the speed and tack
of our hunger to cross the gravid ocean.
Sunlight scatters and dissolves.

Once more before the wind,
we tumble down emerald peaks
on emptied zephyrs and wallow

back to rest among the shells
where seagulls cluck and pick at kelp,
yellow-legs sticky with gravity.

Spinnakered birds sail overhead
half-seen, half-felt,
as legions of stars

rattle the rigging in our ears—
celestial bodies that pull on a loafing sea
that rises only to meet the moon.

Mending

Mending one of those cool shirts
that cost dearly yet does not last,
like the peel of early sunlight
through slatted blinds—

a scissored riddle of rose corduroy,
turquoise stitching and splashes
of velvet—too soon splits
and frays at the shoulder.

Often there's a crack
where bright worlds join—
Japanese pots, repaired with gold.
Slowing the fingers way down,

I tuck under the ragged edge.
My left hand guides and manages
as if not quite conscious—
I've always loved the sinister,

slim and unmarred by hard labor—
the right, silver needle threaded,
fishes and seeks, an eternal repeat,
the seam its purple history.

Not everything needs a mend—
once, I found broken
the leg of a table, and cut the others down
'til it squatted flat, sturdy and new.

I don't say sorry
unless I've hurt someone—
and then, when they sleep,
I enter their dream to apologize.

Genesis

From the beginning, then, with a wink of abandon—
like a trip downtown on an apple-red scooter,

a little crazy on the throttle, steering for the bumps and heaves,
for the joy when it leaps—the flawed engine of our freedom

has been *the word*—I mean, this is just, like, my opinion, man—
but the shout of yay or nay is our yes to play an elusive game,

to choose some fragrant fruit, dangerous and sweet, one of many
mysteries the biome sings today. They say it was woman,

then man, who dined and—right after god created the ocelot,
the unicorn, cilantro (which even then must have tasted

like soap)—brought us the choice to imagine, to *re-word*.
We head for the garden again and again, no longer ashamed

of our nakedness—hey, I'm just one red balloon winding
across a busy sky—and notice the many-gendered angels

arranging some kind of quartet. Listen to the tenor
of their voices, the occasional cymbal crash.

Sherwood Gardens

The dogs of winter have gone, taking their brittle sticks.

Tulips sun labia in public, normal as any folk
as fairies cavort and sing somewhere between hearing and sense
in not-quite harmony—spring's fertile confidence.

Magnolia and worm penetrate—the eye, the tender ground—
strawberries rise and leave their beds, sashay across the lawn,
a slow rainbow of creeping green, then yellow, fattening to red.

The apple tree's pink earrings adorn a couple in love
who kneel and clasp for the camera, as children above in
branches climb to reach the sky, no thought of coming down.

Growing Things

Build a frame around
your garden, bury worry and
the need for a perfect crop,
the right way to plant. Not
liturgy, this box is for angry

shoots that adore the sun's
scorch, that sprout after
deluge, after failures of sting
and decay, early rotted stems
irrelevant by mid-season.

Notice the first tomatoes
begging for applause,
patterns of ripening red
lances of light on the fence,
and outside also the impulse

to beget, a velvet overgrowth
pungent and unstoppable
around your plot of soul—
clover, wood strawberries,
a mess of violets taking over.

Natural Order

Maybe we've had it backwards,
    how we are wounded, heal, and scar.
        Neither muscling through nor creating cover,
            more a visit to the landscape of childhood,
                the path a riot of flora and spider snares,
                    we replant species fragile and tough
                        with due respect for microclimates.
            I eat summer squash and blueberries,
    turn the color of dirt in the sun.
        When thought clears out we are,
            after all, made of the same stuff—
  earth, water, sky, with nowhere to go.
So here it is, the wisdom of the wound—
    once a touch of loud tissue, red
        and uncertain beneath a skin of worry,
            reforested, permits the pleading membrane
            its rugged joy, acquiescing
                just long enough to change.

photograph by R. Kanigel

About the Author

S.B. Merrow is the author of the chapbook *Unpacking the China* (Quills Edge Press, 2016.) Her poems have appeared in *Salamander, Nimrod International Journal, The Tishman Review, Free State Review, Panoply, Passager,* and other journals. A specialist in the field of Boston's traditionally hand-made flutes, she restores and repairs concert flutes for professional flutists, and has contributed essays to *The Flutist Quarterly.* Originally from New England, she lives in Baltimore with her husband, Robert Kanigel.

Kelsay Books

www.ingramcontent.com/pod-product-compliance
Lightning Source LLC
Chambersburg PA
CBHW031149090426
42738CB00008B/1269